AF429305

# AI Driven Incidence Response

Valarian Couch

Published by Valarian Couch, 2023.

While every precaution has been taken in the preparation of this book, the publisher assumes no responsibility for errors or omissions, or for damages resulting from the use of the information contained herein.

AI DRIVEN INCIDENCE RESPONSE

**First edition. December 27, 2023.**

Copyright © 2023 Valarian Couch.

ISBN: 979-8223263524

Written by Valarian Couch.

# AI -Driven Incidence Response
*Accelerating Cybersecurity Incident Handling*

---

## Author's Name: Valarian Couch

# Copyright © 2023 by Valarian Couch

All rights reserved. No part of this publication may be reproduced, distributed, or transmitted in any form or by any means, including photocopying, recording, or other electronic or mechanical methods, without the prior written permission of the publisher, except in the case of brief quotations embodied in critical reviews and certain other noncommercial uses permitted by copyright law.

For permission requests, write to the publisher at the address below.
*[valariancouch@gmail.com]*

# Foreword

In the dynamic and ever-evolving world of cybersecurity, the advent of Artificial Intelligence (AI) has been a game-changer. As we navigate through the complexities of cyber threats and security measures, it becomes clear that traditional methods are no longer enough. This is where AI-driven incident response becomes not just relevant, but essential.

This book, "AI-Driven Incidence Response: Accelerating Cybersecurity Incident Handling," offers a fresh perspective on how AI is revolutionizing the way we handle cyber incidents. The aim is not to overwhelm you with jargon or complex theories, but rather to provide a clear, accessible guide on how AI is transforming cybersecurity.

What makes AI so essential in this field? It's simple: *speed and efficiency*. AI systems can analyze data and identify threats much faster than any human team. This speed is critical in a domain where every second counts. But it's not just about being fast. AI brings a level of precision and foresight that was previously unattainable, predicting and mitigating risks before they become full-blown crises.

Throughout this book, you'll find real-world examples, straightforward explanations, and practical insights. Whether you're a cybersecurity expert or just beginning to explore this field, the content is crafted to resonate with you. We'll dive into how AI algorithms work in detecting and responding to threats, and how you can integrate these technologies into your own cybersecurity strategies.

Remember, this book is not just about understanding the technicalities of AI in cybersecurity. It's about appreciating the human element behind these technologies — the creativity, the innovation, and the dedication of those who work tirelessly to make our digital world safer.

As you turn these pages, I invite you to join us on this journey of discovery and innovation. Let's explore how AI-driven incident response is not just a technological advancement, but a leap forward in protecting our digital lives.

*[Valarian Couch]*

# Acknowledgments

Writing this book has been an incredible journey, and it wouldn't have been possible without the support and encouragement of many people.

First and foremost, I want to express my deepest gratitude to my family. Your unwavering belief in my vision and constant support provided the foundation upon which this book was built. To my wife, for your patience and love, and to my children, who remind me every day of the importance of pursuing one's passions – thank you from the bottom of my heart.

A special thanks goes to my colleagues and peers in the cybersecurity and AI communities. Your insights, feedback, and spirited discussions have been invaluable. I am particularly grateful to my mentor in late memory of Anthony Brown, whose mentorship and wisdom have been guiding lights in my career. Your perspective on the evolving world of cybersecurity has been a major inspiration for this book.

Lastly, to you, the readers, who share a keen interest in the world of AI and cybersecurity – this book is for you. Your eagerness to learn and evolve in this ever-changing field is what drives authors like myself to share our knowledge and experiences. I hope this book provides you with valuable insights and aids in your journey in cybersecurity.

*Thank you all for being part of this incredible journey.*
*VALARIAN COUCH*

# Introduction to AI-Driven Incident Response

The landscape of cyber threats is changing swiftly, and there's a significant uptick in the frequency of attacks that organization/enterprises encounter. Given the worldwide deficit of approximately 3.4 million proficient cybersecurity experts, it's crucial for companies to enhance both the efficiency and effectiveness of their security strategies.

Artificial Intelligence (AI) and Machine Learning (ML) have revolutionized various sectors, including the realm of incident response. These advanced technologies utilize extensive datasets, empowering organizations to identify threats and tackle security incidents instantaneously. AI and ML-driven, automated response systems surpass traditional manual methods in terms of speed and accuracy, reducing the likelihood of human errors. AI-driven incident response is a sophisticated blend of technology and strategy, leveraging artificial intelligence to enhance cybersecurity measures. At its core, it involves employing AI systems to detect, analyze, and respond to cybersecurity incidents more efficiently and effectively than traditional methods.

## The Role of Human Analysts

Though AI and ML technologies provide substantial advantages, the importance of human analysts in the incident detection and response process cannot be understated. Their distinct skills enhance AI/ML's effectiveness. Human analysts contribute invaluable critical thinking, specific domain knowledge, and intuitive understanding. This combination enables them to grasp the broader context, subtle details, and underlying intentions in security incidents, making their role indispensable.

Human experts excel in deciphering the insights produced by AI/ML systems, leveraging their knowledge to authenticate and situate these findings. Their deep grasp of the organization's systems, network infrastructure, and threat environment empowers them to make educated decisions. These analysts are particularly skilled at recognizing false positives, adding depth to incident analyses, and conducting thorough investigations necessitating inventive problem-solving.

## The Role of Artificial Intelligence in Modern Cybersecurity

The role of AI in modern cybersecurity is crucial and multifaceted, significantly enhancing how we protect our digital environments. Unlike traditional methods that often involve manual monitoring and reactive measures, AI introduces a proactive and dynamic approach to security.

*Exploring How AI Transforms Cybersecurity:*

1. **Constant Network Watch**: AI excels in keeping an eye on vast networks all the time. It checks data flows, quickly spotting anything odd. This ongoing vigilance helps catch threats early, way faster than humans can.
2. **Predicting and Preparing for Threats**: AI's knack for predicting upcoming dangers is remarkable. It looks at past data, spots patterns, and can guess where future attacks might happen. This lets organizations strengthen their defenses before anything bad occurs instead of just reacting when it's too late.

3. **Quick Automatic Reaction to Threats**: When AI finds a threat, it acts fast. It can isolate systems in danger, block sketchy network activity, or immediately fix weak spots. This quick action leaves little room for attackers to do damage.

4. **Spotting Hidden Patterns**: AI is great at finding hidden data patterns that people might miss. This skill is key in noticing complex cyber-attacks that try to slip past usual security. AI can spot these sneaky threats, like advanced attacks or new, unknown threats.

5. **Always Learning and Improving**: AI in cybersecurity gets smarter over time. It learns from new information and adjusts. As threats get trickier, AI becomes better at spotting and stopping them.

6. **Boosting Human Efforts**: AI doesn't replace cybersecurity experts but supports them. It takes care of the regular checks and analysis, letting humans tackle tougher problems like planning defenses and digging into complex attacks. This teamwork between people and AI makes cybersecurity much stronger.

# Chapter 1

# Understanding Cybersecurity Incidents

# Intro

In the digital age, understanding cybersecurity incidents is crucial. These incidents are not just minor glitches; they're serious threats that can have far-reaching consequences.

# What are Cybersecurity Incidents?

A cybersecurity incident is any event that threatens the security of information systems. Think of it as a break-in but in the digital world. These incidents can take many forms, such as viruses, malware attacks, hacking, and data breaches. They can target anybody (from individuals to large corporations and even governments).

## Cybersecurity incidents according to their criticality

On the other hand, cybersecurity incidents can be classified by their criticality, understanding this as the impact they have on the information, systems, and networks they affect. The levels of criticality or priority in cybersecurity incidents can be classified into three, both for critical infrastructures and for other agents, companies, and citizens:

1. High criticality level: group together incidents that affect systems or information critical to the entity and potentially impact the business.
2. Medium criticality level: these include incidents that affect systems or information that are not critical for the entity or whose impact does not directly impact the development of the business.
3. Low criticality level: Refers to incidents in systems with a low level of importance, investigations that involve forensic analyses that last over time, or generic security queries. < /span>.

# Types of Incidents

Let's look at some common types of cybersecurity incidents:

- **DoS and DDoS Attacks**

A DoS (denial-of-service) attack floods a system with too much traffic, making it unable to handle real requests. A DDoS (distributed denial-of-service) attack does the same but uses many infected computers. These attacks stop a site from working, sometimes shutting it down completely. Unlike other cyber-attacks that let hackers break into systems, DoS and DDoS attacks just stop a service from working. Sometimes, a DoS attack can also make a system weak to other attacks. A big example is the 2020 attack on Amazon Web Services.

- **MITM Attacks**

MITM (man-in-the-middle) attacks let hackers listen to conversations between two parties. The hacker secretly changes or reads messages without the parties knowing. Protecting against this includes using strong encryption or a VPN (virtual private network).

- **Phishing Attacks**

Phishing attacks trick people with emails that look like they're from trusted sources. The goal is to steal sensitive info. These attacks often use fake links to install malware or get personal details. Being cautious about the emails you open and the links you click can help prevent these attacks.

- **Whale-phishing Attacks**

These target companies' big shots, like CEOs, to get valuable info. If these high-level people download ransomware, they might pay to keep it quiet. Avoiding these attacks is similar to regular phishing: check emails and links carefully.

- **Spear-phishing Attacks**

Spear phishing is like phishing but more targeted. The attacker researches and sends messages that seem very relevant to the target. The email might look like it's from someone the target knows and trusts. Always check email details and avoid clicking on unknown links.

- **Ransomware**

This is when hackers lock your system and ask for money. You pay, and they tell you how to get your computer back. They call it ransomware because it's like a ransom. Hackers put this into your computer through websites or email attachments. It finds weak spots that are not fixed by the maker or IT team. The malware locks your computer or even many in a business. Sometimes, it waits before locking everything at once. It can spread through the network or USB drives. Some ransomware is sneaky and avoids antivirus software. Be careful online and use advanced firewalls with AI to stop it.

- **Password Attack**

Getting your password is a big goal for hackers. They might find it on a note at your desk or pay someone inside for it. They could also grab it from unencrypted network transmissions or trick you into giving it. Some just guess, especially if it's simple like "1234567." Hackers use brute-force attacks, guessing passwords based on personal info or dictionary attacks with common words. Protect yourself with a lockout policy that blocks access after too many wrong tries. Change your password if locked out. Hackers might note failed passwords and guess right next time.

- **SQL Injection Attack**

This targets websites with databases. Hackers send a command from their computer to the database server. If it works, they can steal, change, or delete data or even shut down the database. Protect yourself by limiting who can access important databases.

- **URL Interpretation**

Hackers change URLs to get to restricted data. They might guess admin page URLs and try simple or known passwords to get in. Protect your website with strong authentication, like multi-factor authentication.

- **DNS Spoofing**

Here, hackers redirect you to a fake website. You might give away sensitive info there. They can also use it to harm a company's reputation. Keep your DNS servers updated to avoid this.

- **Session Hijacking**

This is when hackers take over an online session by replacing the real user's IP address with theirs. The server doesn't notice and keeps talking to the hacker. Use a VPN to keep sessions secure.

- **Brute force attack**

A brute-force attack is named for its straightforward approach. Here, the attacker keeps guessing login details until they find the right one and break into the system. Although it seems like a lot of effort, attackers often use automated bots to speed up the guessing process. They feed these bots a bunch of possible passwords and let them try each one. When the bot hits the correct password, the attacker gets access.

To stop these attacks, it's good to have a system that locks someone out after they get the password wrong too many times. This lockout works even if someone tries from a different computer or internet connection. Another tip is to use really random passwords. Avoid common words, dates, or number sequences. For example, cracking a 10-digit random password could take years, even for sophisticated guessing software.

- **Web Attacks**

Web attacks are tricks used to take advantage of weaknesses in websites and online applications. Imagine every time you use a website, like for online banking, you're giving it instructions. For example, when you transfer money, you're telling the website to move money from your account to someone else's. Hackers find ways to misuse these instructions for their own gain.

Some usual web attacks are SQL injection and cross-site scripting (XSS), which we'll talk more about later. Hackers also use tricks like cross-site request forgery (CSRF) and messing with website parameters. In a CSRF attack, hackers' trick someone into doing something that helps the hacker. For instance, they might make you click on a link that secretly changes your login details for a website. Then, the hacker can use these new details to log in as if they were you.

Parameter tampering is when someone messes with the settings that developers put in place to keep certain operations safe. The way these operations work depends on the input in these settings. An attacker can just change these settings, getting around the security that was relying on them.

To protect your websites from attacks, you should regularly check and fix any weak spots in your web apps. One good fix that doesn't slow down your website is using anti-CSRF tokens. These tokens are like secret handshakes between the user's browser and your website. Before any action is done, the website checks if the token is right. If it is, the action is allowed; if not, it's stopped. Another tool is SameSite flags, which only let requests from the same website go through. This makes any website set up by an attacker useless.

- **Insider Threats**

Often, the biggest security threats to a company come from its own employees. These individuals usually have access to many systems and sometimes even have special permissions, like admin rights, which let them alter important system settings or security rules. Also, because they know a lot about the company's cybersecurity setup and how it responds to dangers, they can figure out ways to enter areas they shouldn't, change security settings, or choose the perfect time to launch an attack.

In addition, people working in a company usually know a lot about its Cybersecurity architecture and how it handles online dangers. They might use this knowledge to get into restricted areas, change security settings, or figure out the best time to attack.

A good way to stop these insider threats is to let employees who really need it access important computer systems. And for those few who do need access, use something called MFA. This means they have to use something they know (like a password) and something they have (like a USB stick) to get into these systems. For example, they might need to type a password and plug in a USB stick or use a special number from a device they carry. They can only get in if both the password and the number are right.

Though Multi-Factor Authentication (MFA) doesn't stop every attack, it helps identify attackers, especially since only a few people can access sensitive areas. This limited access acts as a deterrent. If someone within your organization tries to commit cybercrime, it's easier to figure out who it is due to the small number of people who could be responsible.

- **Trojan Horses**

A Trojan horse attack is like a trick where bad software is hidden inside what looks like a good program. When someone uses this program, thinking it's safe, the hidden bad software (malware) can create a secret way for hackers to get into the computer or network. It's named after the Greek story where soldiers hid in a wooden horse to sneak into Troy. Like the Trojans brought the horse inside their city, not knowing soldiers were inside, a person might let a harmful app into their system without realizing it's dangerous.

To avoid these attacks, people should only download or install things from trusted sources. Also, using advanced firewalls can help check incoming data for any signs of these Trojans. Also, (Next-Generation Firewalls) NGFWs are designed to inspect data packets to check for possible Trojan threats.

Next-Generation Firewalls these are a type of firewall that provides more advanced security features than traditional firewalls. Next-generation firewalls can inspect and filter traffic more deeply, including examining the contents of data packets, not just the headers. They typically include features like intrusion prevention systems (IPS), the ability to identify and control applications (not just port numbers), advanced threat protection against malware, and sometimes even the capability to integrate with other security systems for improved threat intelligence and response.

- **Drive-by Attacks**

In a drive-by attack, a hacker puts harmful code on a not-so-secure website. If you go to that website, this bad code automatically runs on your computer and causes harm. It's called "drive-by" because you get infected just by visiting the website without having to click on anything or type in any info.

To stay safe from these attacks, you should keep your computer and all your programs, like Adobe Acrobat and Flash, updated. They are often used when you're online. Also, using web-filtering software helps. It can tell if a website is dangerous before you even visit it.

- **XSS Attacks**

In cross-site scripting, also known as XSS, an attacker sends harmful scripts through clickable things like links. These scripts go to the victim's web browser. When the person clicks on these, the bad script starts working. This happens when they're already logged into a website, so the website thinks whatever is entered is okay and normal. But really, the script has been changed by the attacker, causing the website to do something it shouldn't, thinking it's the user's action.

For example, imagine someone sneaking into your online bank transfer. They secretly switch the name on your transfer form to their own and might even increase the amount of money you're sending. So, instead of sending money to the person you meant to, it goes to the hacker, possibly more than you planned to send.

A simple method to stop XSS attacks is to make a list of safe items that are allowed. If something isn't on this list, the web application won't accept it. Another method is called cleaning. This involves looking at the information being put in and making sure it doesn't have anything dangerous in it.

- **Eavesdropping Attacks**

In eavesdropping attacks, a wrongdoer secretly intercepts data flowing through a network. They can grab sensitive details like usernames, passwords, and even credit card information. These attacks happen in two ways: active and passive.

During an active eavesdropping attack, the hacker puts special software in the network's path to snatch and examine the data for valuable information. On the other hand, in a passive eavesdropping attack, the hacker simply 'overhears' the data being sent, searching for any useful information to steal.

Both active and passive eavesdropping are forms of middleman attacks. A great method to stop these is to encrypt your data. This makes sure a hacker can't use your information, whether they're actively or passively listening in.

- **Birthday Attack**

In a birthday attack, a hacker takes advantage of a key security tool called hash algorithms. These algorithms help confirm if messages are genuine by using a digital signature. When someone receives a message, they check this signature to ensure it's real. But if a hacker manages to make a hash that looks exactly like the original sender's, they can swap the real message with their fake one. The receiver's system will think it's legit because the hash matches.

The term "birthday attack" comes from the birthday paradox. This paradox shows that in a group of 23 people, there's a pretty good chance two of them share the same birthday. It's surprising because most of us think our birthdays are unique. Similarly, hashes may seem unique, but they're not always as distinctive as we believe.

To avoid these kinds of attacks, it's best to use longer hashes. Adding just one extra digit to a hash makes it way harder for someone to come up with a match.

- **Malware Attack**

Malware is a name for harmful/malicious software. It messes up how a computer works, damages data, or secretly watches what you're doing online. This bad software can move from one gadget to another or just stay on one and cause trouble there. Many types of cyberattacks use malware, like those where hackers intercept your data, trick you into giving information, lock your files for money, sneakily insert harmful code, or launch surprise attacks when you visit certain websites.

In a malware attack, you need to download the harmful software onto your device. This happens when you, the user, do something like clicking a link or downloading a file. To protect yourself, it's not just about having firewalls that can spot this bad software. It's also important to learn what kind of software you shouldn't download, which links to double-check before clicking, and which emails and attachments to stay away from.

- **Data Breaches:**

When confidential information is accessed without permission, it's a data breach. This can happen through hacking, lost or stolen devices, or inadvertent exposure by employees.

# The Consequences of Cybersecurity Incidents

The consequences of these incidents can be significant:

1. Financial Loss: Both individuals and organizations can suffer severe financial damages due to theft, fraud, or the costs of responding to an incident.
2. Reputational Damage: For businesses, when a company faces a cyber-attack, it can lose its customers' trust and damage its brand.
3. Operational Disruption: Incidents can disrupt normal business operations, leading to loss of productivity and service availability.
4. Legal and Regulatory Consequences: There could be legal penalties for failure to protect sensitive data, especially if the data involves the personal information of customers or employees.
5. Personal Impact: For individuals, these incidents can mean the loss of personal, financial, or sensitive data, leading to potential identity theft and privacy violations.

# Why It Matters

Understanding what constitutes a cybersecurity incident is crucial in today's interconnected world. As our reliance on digital technology grows, so does the potential for these incidents to occur. Being aware of the different types of incidents, how they can happen, and their potential impact is the first step in developing effective strategies to prevent and respond to these digital threats.

# Chapter 2

# The Basics of Incident Response

# Introduction

In this chapter, we'll dive into the essentials of incident response in the world of cybersecurity. Think of incident response like a fire brigade for cyber-attacks – it's all about how to act fast and effectively when things go wrong in the digital realm.

# What Is Incident Response?

Incident response refers to how an organization deals with a data breach or a cyberattack. This includes how they control the fallout from the attack or breach (the "incident"). The main aim is to handle the incident in a way that keeps damage, recovery time, and costs low and also minimizes other negative effects like harm to the company's reputation.

Every organization needs a straightforward plan for handling incidents. This plan must explain what counts as an incident for the company and lay out a step-by-step process for dealing with one. It's also important to clearly identify which teams, staff members, or leaders are in charge of overseeing the incident response and who will carry out each step in the plan.

There are several approaches to building a structured IR process:

1. NIST process: The National Institute of Standards and Technology (NIST) breaks down incident response into four stages: preparation, detection and analysis, containment, eradication and recovery, and post-incident activity.

2. SANS process: The SANS Institute suggests a six-step method for

incident response: preparation, identification, containment, eradication, recovery, and lessons learned.

3. Seven-Step Approach: Some experts in cybersecurity recommend a seven-step process. This includes all the previous steps plus regular re-testing and training to keep the organization prepared and alert.

# Who Handles Incident Responses?

Incident response, a crucial task in any organization, is typically managed by a team known as the Computer Incident Response Team (CIRT), which can also be referred to as a cyber incident response team. This team is usually made up of a diverse group of professionals. It includes security experts and general IT staff, who are the technical backbone of the team. In addition, there are also members from legal, human resources, and public relations departments. These individuals bring a range of expertise to handle various aspects of an incident.

According to the insights from Gartner, a CIRT is essentially a dedicated group tasked with tackling security breaches, viruses, and other serious incidents, especially in companies that are highly vulnerable to such security threats. The team doesn't just consist of technical experts who are proficient in neutralizing specific threats but also includes specialists who can advise the company's top executives on the best ways to communicate about these incidents. This communication strategy is vital in managing the company's public image and internal morale in the aftermath of security incidents.

In simpler terms, a CIRT is like a specialized emergency response team within a company, equipped not only to fight off digital threats but also to help the company navigate through the aftermath effectively.

# Six Steps for Effective Incident Response

The Six Steps of Incident Response

1. Preparation   3. Containment   5. Recovery

2. Identification   4. Eradication   6. Lessons Learned

- **Preparation:**

The key step in responding to a security incident is getting ready for a breach that's bound to happen at some point. This preparation phase is crucial as it shows how effectively the company's Cyber Incident Response Team (CIRT) can handle a crisis. This stage includes setting up policies, planning out the response strategy, organizing communication methods, keeping detailed records, selecting the team members for the CIRT, managing who has access to what, deciding on the necessary tools, and providing adequate training to the team.

- **Identification:**

Identification refers to the method of quickly recognizing incidents so that a fast reaction can be initiated, helping to cut down on expenses and damage. In this crucial phase of responding to incidents efficiently, IT personnel collect a variety of data from different sources. This includes information from log files, various monitoring tools, error alerts, systems that detect unauthorized access, and firewall activities. They do this not only to spot incidents as they happen but also to understand how widespread or serious these incidents are.

- **Containment:**

When a problem comes up, our first job is to stop it from getting worse. Catching the issue early, as mentioned in step two, helps us control it quickly and reduce harm. It's crucial to remember that following all of SANS' advice during this stage is important. This is especially true for making sure we don't lose any evidence that might be needed for legal reasons later on. The steps we need to follow include initially containing the problem in the short term, backing up the system, and then making sure the issue is fully under control for the long term. This approach ensures that the damage is limited and that any potential legal actions are supported by preserving necessary evidence.

- **Eradication:**

Eradication, an essential stage in successful incident response, involves getting rid of the threat and bringing the impacted systems back to how they were before, aiming to keep data loss as low as possible. It's crucial to verify that the right actions have been carried out up to this point. These actions include not just deleting the harmful elements but also making sure that the systems impacted are thoroughly cleansed. This step is about ensuring the complete removal of the threat and restoring normal functionality to the systems, with a focus on maintaining the integrity of the data involved.

- **Recovery:**

The key focus of this stage in responding to an incident involves a thorough check-up of systems before they are reintroduced into regular operation. This is to make sure they haven't been infected again or still carry any security threats. This process includes several important steps. Firstly, deciding when to get everything up and running again is crucial. Then, we need to rigorously test the systems that were previously compromised, keeping an eye out for any unusual or suspicious activities. In addition, this stage involves using specialized tools to test, monitor, and confirm that the system's behavior is normal and safe. In simpler terms, think of it like a doctor who not only treats a patient but also keeps checking them regularly to ensure they stay healthy and don't fall sick again.

- **Lessons Learned:**

Lessons learned is an essential part of handling incidents, as it plays a vital role in teaching and enhancing how future incidents are managed. During this stage, organizations get a chance to refine their plans for responding to incidents by incorporating insights that might not have been evident when the incident occurred. They also complete thorough documentation, which serves as a valuable resource for handling similar situations in the future. The reports generated from the lessons learned offer a detailed analysis of the entire incident. These reports are not only useful in debriefing sessions but also serve as educational tools for new members of the Critical Incident Response Team (CIRT). Additionally, they act as standards for evaluating and comparing the effectiveness of responses to different incidents. This process is crucial because it ensures that organizations are better prepared and more resilient in the face of future challenges.

# What Is an Incident Response Plan (IRP)?

An incident response plan consists of a carefully crafted set of instructions outlining the necessary actions for each stage of responding to an incident. This plan should clearly outline who is responsible for what, how communication should be handled, and what the standard procedures are for responding. It's crucial to use straightforward, unambiguous language in your plan. This includes clearly defining commonly misunderstood terms such as "event," "alert," and "incident." To avoid confusion, it's advisable to use these terms in a specific and consistent manner throughout your plan. This approach ensures everyone involved understands their roles and the steps to be taken, promoting an effective and coordinated response to any incidents. In your plan, consider these terms and their specific applications like this:

- "Event" refers to any modification in your system's settings, its current status, or how it communicates. This could be something like a request made to a server, updating access permissions, or even removing some data.
- "Alert" is a kind of message you get because of an event. These alerts can either flag something unusual or just highlight ordinary activities that need your attention. Think of it as getting a heads-up about a rarely used network port suddenly becoming active or a warning when your storage space is starting to run low.
- "Incident" is a more serious term. It's used for events that actually threaten the security or integrity of your system. Examples of incidents are when someone's login credentials get stolen or when harmful software, like malware, gets installed on your system.

# Why is a Good Incident Response Plan Essential?

A good incident response (IR) plan is much like a well-rehearsed emergency drill, crucial for the swift and effective handling of cybersecurity incidents. Its importance cannot be overstated, as it serves several vital functions.

Firstly, a robust IR plan is instrumental in minimizing the damage from a cyber incident. Like a fire escape plan in a building, it guides immediate and effective action, reducing the impact of the attack. This rapid response is not only essential for protecting sensitive data but also for maintaining operational integrity.

Moreover, cyber incidents can be financially draining, consuming significant time and resources. A well-crafted response plan can cut down these costs dramatically. It streamlines the process of identifying, containing, and resolving the incident, thereby saving money and resources that might otherwise be spent in a prolonged recovery process.

Another critical aspect is the plan's role in recovery time. The faster an organization can bounce back from a cyber incident, the less downtime it will experience, which is crucial for maintaining business continuity and customer trust. This quick recovery is especially important in today's fast-paced digital environment, where even a short period of downtime can lead to significant losses and eroded customer confidence.

Compliance is also a key consideration. Many industries are governed by regulations that mandate the need for a formal IR plan. Without a comprehensive and compliant response plan, organizations may face legal and regulatory repercussions, adding to the challenges posed by the cyber incident itself.

The plan also plays a pivotal role in protecting an organization's reputation. In the digital age, news of a cyber breach can spread rapidly, and the manner in which a company responds is often scrutinized. An effective and efficient response can help manage the situation better, safeguarding the company's public image.

Furthermore, a good IR plan isn't just about responding to incidents; it's about learning from them. By analyzing past incidents and current threats, an organization can gain a deeper understanding of the cybersecurity landscape. This ongoing analysis is crucial for staying ahead of potential threats and fortifying defenses.

Finally, the essence of a good IR plan lies in its ability to facilitate continuous improvement. Each incident, regardless of its scale, provides valuable insights. A robust plan includes mechanisms for capturing these lessons and integrating them into future strategies and responses.

# Chapter 3

# AI In Cybersecurity: An Overview

# AI and Machine Learning Concepts in Cybersecurity

The first step to establishing the best defense against a potential cyber-attack is to incorporate a solution that includes preventive monitoring, user education, and adequate patching and incident management.

In today's digital world, cybersecurity is like a never-ending battle against hackers and cyber threats. To stay ahead in this battle, we're turning to Artificial Intelligence (AI) and Machine Learning (ML). But what exactly are these technologies, and how do they help us?

# Artificial Intelligence in Cybersecurity

Artificial Intelligence (AI) refers to systems that are trained to carry out certain jobs without the need for direct programming. This characteristic enables AI to greatly enhance the analysis and learning of data in cybersecurity solutions. As a result, AI is rapidly becoming a top focus for IT departments within organizations, as it offers more effective and accurate ways to handle cybersecurity challenges. This shift highlights the increasing reliance on AI to strengthen data protection and improve overall security measures in the digital world.

It is a technology in constant evolution, and its algorithms allow machine learning, known as machine learning, which helps the system learn patterns and adapt to simplify responding to incident risks.

Cybersecurity professionals are inundated with many tasks, excess data, lack of time, and low availability of skills, so AI can have a great impact on IT managers by allowing:

- Accurately detect threats
- Automate the response
- Streamline attack investigation

This is one of the most important benefits since human resources in cybersecurity are not yet able to meet the demand, and in this way, the efforts of administrators can be optimized.

AI systems collaborate by categorizing attacks according to the threat level. Those in charge of cybersecurity, for their part, assign the priority with which each one should be addressed, starting with the most dangerous for the state of the company's information.

Malware attacks and similar threats are constantly advancing, becoming quicker and more complex. That's why using machine learning is crucial to keep up with these challenges.

## Machine learning

Today, most of the relevant research and advances in the cybersecurity industry come from the AI subdiscipline called machine learning, which focuses on the application of algorithms in relation to data.

In the world of AI and cybersecurity, we mainly see two types of approaches: ones that are decided by human experts and ones that are determined by computers themselves.

Analysts create protocols and rules based on their experience; however, they may run into problems when a new or unknown threat appears.

For their part, the machines apply their security protocols according to the information acquired by machine learning and deep learning, in which they directly influence behavioral patterns in networks to predict future movements and attacks; the operating systems used, as well as the servers, firewalls, security actions users and response tactics. These technologies are crucial because cyber threats are becoming more sophisticated. Traditional security tools follow preset rules, but hackers constantly find new ways to break these rules. AI and

ML adapt and learn, making them powerful tools for detecting and stopping new kinds of cyberattacks.

## Real-Life Examples of AI/ML in Incident Detection

> Large financial institutions like big banks use AI systems to watch over their computer networks. This AI spotted weird activity that looked like a cyber-attack. Thanks to this, the bank's security team was able to act fast and stop any major harm from happening.

> A company specializing in online security created an AI tool to find and stop new types of computer viruses. This tool, which learns by examining how files act, was able to catch and block complex virus attacks, helping to defend against new and changing online threats.

# Benefits of AI in Detecting and Preventing Cyber Incidents

The integration of AI in cybersecurity has revolutionized the way we approach digital defense. Here's a more detailed look at the benefits:

**Enhanced Detection Capabilities:** AI's ability to process and analyze vast amounts of data quickly surpasses human capacity. This rapid processing enables the early detection of potential threats, even those that are subtle or complex. AI systems can sift through data at an unprecedented rate, identifying patterns and anomalies that could indicate a breach or an impending attack. This swift detection is crucial in a domain where every second counts.

**Proactive Threat Intelligence:** Traditional cybersecurity methods tend to be reactive, focusing on threats only after they have been identified. AI, on the other hand, offers a proactive approach. By continuously learning from new data and past incidents, AI can anticipate and identify potential vulnerabilities and attack vectors. This proactive stance not only prevents known threats but also helps in predicting and preparing for future attack methodologies.

**Adaptive Learning and Evolution:** One of the most significant benefits of AI in cybersecurity is its ability to learn and evolve. Through machine learning algorithms, AI systems continually update their knowledge base with information from recent cyber incidents. This constant learning process means that AI-driven cybersecurity solutions are always up-to-date, adapting to the latest tactics employed by cybercriminals and thus remaining effective against even the most novel attacks.

**Reducing False Positives:** False positives are a significant challenge in cybersecurity, where legitimate activities are mistakenly flagged as threats, leading to wasted resources and potential disruption. AI's advanced algorithms are far more adept at distinguishing between genuine threats and benign anomalies compared to traditional systems. This precision reduces the number of false positives, ensuring that security teams focus their efforts on actual threats.

**Automated Response and Remediation:** AI can not only detect threats but also respond to them autonomously. In many cases, AI-driven systems can implement immediate countermeasures to mitigate or contain the impact of a cyberattack. This capability is especially valuable in scenarios where a rapid response is crucial to prevent extensive damage.

**Scalability and Flexibility:** Cyber threats are constantly evolving, and AI systems are uniquely suited to scale and adapt to these changes. Whether dealing with increasing volumes of data, new types of cyber threats, or expanding network infrastructures, AI-driven cybersecurity solutions can adjust and expand their capabilities accordingly.

**Cost-effectiveness:** By automating detection and response processes, AI reduces the need for large security teams to monitor and analyze data continuously. This automation can lead to significant cost savings for organizations, allowing them to allocate resources more efficiently.

**Enhanced Collaboration and Knowledge Sharing:** AI systems can facilitate better collaboration and knowledge sharing among cybersecurity professionals. By processing and synthesizing information from various sources, AI can provide insights that might not be apparent through human analysis alone, fostering a more collaborative and informed approach to cybersecurity.

# Use Cases of Artificial Intelligence in Security

AI offers many possibilities for security. For instance:

- For individual device protection, AI can examine how users and programs act to spot signs of hacked accounts or viruses.
- Network security: AI can review data flow to find patterns or signals that suggest different kinds of cyber threats.
- Cloud Security: AI solutions can help address common cloud security challenges, such as ensuring cloud permissions, access controls, and security settings are configured correctly.
- Fraud detection: AI systems can analyze user behavior for anomalies or malicious actions that could indicate possible fraud.

# Best practices for
# implementing AI in security

AI is a powerful tool, but it can also be dangerous if used incorrectly. When designing and implementing AI-based security solutions, it is important to consider the following best practices.

- **Develop an AI strategy.**

AI is a promising tool for security. It is ideal for solving many of the major challenges facing security teams, including large volumes of data, limited resources, and the need to quickly respond to cyber-attacks< a i=2>.

While AI can be helpful for improving security, it's not a magic solution. To make it work well, a crucial step is figuring out how to use AI to tackle a company's security problems and creating a plan to fit AI into the company's security setup and procedures.

- **Ensure data quality and privacy.**

AI is only as good as the data used to train and operate it. An organization can improve the effectiveness of an AI system by providing it with more and higher quality data to provide a more contextual and comprehensive view of an organization's security posture.

Nevertheless, there are some worries associated with how AI uses data. If the data is messed up or wrong, the AI system will end up making wrong choices. Also, if you give sensitive data to the AI system, there's a chance it might get exposed. So, when a company is planning its AI strategy, it needs to think about how to make sure the data is accurate and private when the AI system is running.

- **Building an ethical framework for the use of AI**

AI operates as a "mystery box," and its effectiveness relies on the quality of the data it's trained on. If that data is prejudiced or unjust, the AI model will also reflect these issues.

While AI systems can enhance security measures, it's important to think about and deal with the moral concerns linked to their deployment. For example, if bias in an AI system could negatively affect employees, customers, suppliers, etc., then the AI system should not be used as the final authority in making those decisions.

- **Regularly test and update AI models.**

The quality of an AI system model depends on the data used to train it. If that data is incomplete, biased, or out of date, the internal evaluation system may not make the best decisions.

An organization using AI systems should periodically test and update its models to ensure they are up-to-date and correct. This is especially true when using AI for security, as the rapidly evolving security landscape means that older AI models may be unable to detect newer attacks.

# The Future of AI in Cybersecurity

Artificial Intelligence (AI) is set to play an increasingly significant role in the field of cybersecurity. Let's explore three key ways AI will transform the security landscape:

> The Growth and Improvement of AI and Machine Learning Technologies

While AI and machine learning have made headlines recently, they're still in the early stages of development. As these technologies continue to improve, we can expect them to become more effective and versatile in cybersecurity applications. This means they'll be better at detecting threats, predicting vulnerabilities, and offering solutions to complex security challenges.

> Synergy with Other Cutting-Edge Technologies

AI doesn't exist in a vacuum. It's evolving alongside other groundbreaking technologies, like 5G networks and the Internet of Things (IoT). When AI is integrated with these technologies, it creates exciting possibilities for cybersecurity. For instance, IoT's extensive data collection and remote management, combined with AI's analytical and decision-making process, could lead to more robust and intelligent security systems.

> Changing Dynamics in the Security Industry and labor Market

Just like in other sectors, AI is poised to reshape the security industry and the labor market. As AI starts handling repetitive tasks and enhancing security protocols, human workers in cybersecurity will shift their focus. They'll collaborate more with AI systems, leveraging their capabilities to achieve greater security efficiency on a larger scale. This partnership will not only elevate security standards but also redefine job roles within the industry, offering new opportunities and challenges for professionals.

# Chapter 4

# Ai-Driven Incident Response Mechanisms

In this chapter, we delve into the core of AI-driven incident response mechanisms, focusing on two key aspects: AI algorithms for incident detection and automating response with AI. Our goal is to present these concepts in an accessible and easy-to-understand manner.

# AI Algorithms for Incident Detection

AI algorithms for incident detection are a cornerstone in modern cybersecurity, offering a sophisticated means of identifying potential threats in real time. These algorithms are designed to analyze vast amounts of data from various sources, like network traffic, server logs, and end-point devices, to detect unusual patterns or anomalies that might indicate a security incident.

At the heart of these algorithms is the principle of pattern recognition. AI systems are trained to understand what normal network and system behavior looks like. They achieve this through a process called machine learning, where the algorithm is exposed to a large dataset of historical security incidents and learns to differentiate between normal operations and potential threats.

One of the key strengths of AI in incident detection is its ability to handle the sheer volume and complexity of data that modern networks generate. Traditional security systems often rely on predefined rules or signatures to identify threats. However, with the dynamic and ever-evolving nature of cyber threats, these traditional methods are not always effective. AI, on the other hand, can continuously learn and adapt to new patterns of behavior, making it more effective in identifying novel or sophisticated attacks.

For instance, AI algorithms can detect a range of anomalies, from simple ones like multiple failed login attempts from a single IP address, which could indicate a brute force attack, to more complex scenarios, such as subtle shifts in network traffic, which could suggest data exfiltration by an insider.

Moreover, AI-driven incident detection is not just about identifying known threats; it's also highly effective in uncovering zero-day attacks – new, previously unknown threats that have no defined signatures yet. By analyzing deviations from normal behavior rather than relying on known threat signatures, AI can flag these novel threats.

Another significant aspect is the speed and efficiency of AI algorithms. Cybersecurity incidents require rapid response to minimize damage. AI's ability to process and analyze data in real-time ensures that threats are identified almost as soon as they occur, enabling quicker mitigation and response.

In addition, AI-driven systems are also capable of contextual analysis. This means they can take into account the context in which certain activities occur, adding a layer of sophistication to the detection process. For example, a file transfer happening at an unusual time or a high volume of data being downloaded from a sensitive server can be flagged, considering the context of the activity.

# Automating Response with AI in Cybersecurity

Automating response with AI is a game-changer in the field of cybersecurity. It involves leveraging artificial Intelligence to react quickly and efficiently to security threats, minimizing the time between detection and response.

*key aspects of automating response with Artificial Intelligence*

> **Instantaneous Reaction**

Instantaneous reaction in AI-driven cybersecurity is a transformative feature that greatly enhances an organization's ability to defend against cyber threats. This aspect of AI technology allows for immediate detection and response to potential security incidents, providing a crucial edge in the fast-paced realm of cyber defense.

AI systems are designed to operate at speeds far surpassing human capabilities, particularly in identifying and reacting to threats. These systems can analyze vast amounts of data and identify suspicious activities in milliseconds. This rapid processing means that as soon as a threat is detected, whether it's a malware infiltration, a network breach, or an unusual data transfer, the AI system can instantly initiate a response.

This kind of swift reaction is especially critical when dealing with sophisticated cyber-attacks like ransomware or phishing attempts, which can spread rapidly and cause significant damage in a short period. By responding immediately, AI systems help to prevent these attacks from escalating, reducing the potential harm significantly.

Moreover, the capability of AI for instantaneous reaction is not just limited to reactive measures. AI systems can also be proactive, identifying and mitigating potential threats before they materialize into actual attacks. By constantly analyzing patterns and network behaviors, AI can anticipate vulnerabilities and reinforce defenses preemptively, further enhancing an organization's security posture.

The continuous operation of AI systems ensures round-the-clock monitoring and protection. This is particularly beneficial in scenarios where human monitoring is not feasible due to the scale of data or operational demands. AI's ability to tirelessly monitor and instantly respond is a critical asset in maintaining robust cybersecurity defenses.

Additionally, the instantaneous reaction feature of AI in cybersecurity is a key factor in minimizing the spread and impact of attacks. By quickly isolating affected systems or blocking malicious traffic, AI helps contain the threat, limiting its reach and mitigating its consequences.

### › Dynamic Response Strategies

Dynamic response strategies in AI-driven cybersecurity are pivotal because they allow the system to adapt its responses based on the specific characteristics of each detected threat. This adaptability is crucial for effectively countering a wide range of cyber threats.

- Tailored Responses to Specific Threats:

AI systems are programmed to recognize different types of cybersecurity incidents, such as malware attacks, data breaches, or unauthorized access attempts. Based on the nature and severity of the threat, the AI chooses an appropriate response. For instance, in the case of malware detection, the system might automatically isolate the infected files or systems to prevent the spread of the virus.

- Predictive Analysis and Pre-emptive Measures:

Beyond reacting to existing threats, dynamic response strategies often include predictive analysis. AI algorithms analyze patterns and trends in data to predict potential vulnerabilities or upcoming attacks. This allows organizations to strengthen their defenses proactively in areas identified as high-risk, potentially preventing attacks before they occur.

- Scalability of Responses:

AI-driven systems are capable of scaling their responses based on the extent of the threat. For a small-scale intrusion, the response might be to simply block a specific user or IP address. However, for a large-scale, sophisticated attack, the system might initiate a series of complex actions like rerouting traffic, shutting down certain operations, or triggering a comprehensive system-wide security audit.

- Context-Aware Decision Making:

One of the strengths of AI in cybersecurity is its ability to make context-aware decisions. By analyzing the context in which a threat is detected — such as time of day, network traffic patterns, and user behavior — AI can determine the likelihood of a false positive and adjust its response accordingly. This reduces unnecessary disruptions caused by overreactions to benign anomalies.

- Real-Time Adjustment:

Dynamic response strategies are not static; they adjust in real-time. As an attack unfolds, the AI system continuously analyzes incoming data and modifies its response accordingly. This agility ensures that the system remains effective even as the nature of the attack changes.

- Integration with Incident Response Teams:

AI-driven responses are often designed to work in conjunction with human incident response teams. The AI can handle the immediate, automated responses while providing critical information and analysis to the human team, who can then make more nuanced decisions and take strategic actions based on the AI's inputs.

### › Reducing Workload and Errors

Reducing workload and errors through AI-driven automation in cybersecurity is a crucial aspect of modern incident response strategies. This approach involves using artificial Intelligence to handle routine and repetitive tasks, which not only accelerates the process but also enhances accuracy and consistency.

- Handling Repetitive Tasks:

In the realm of cybersecurity, many tasks are repetitive and time-consuming, such as monitoring network traffic, scanning for vulnerabilities, or sorting through false positives in threat detection. AI can efficiently manage these tasks, operating around the clock without the fatigue or lapses in concentration that can affect human operators. This constant vigilance ensures that threats are not overlooked and are dealt with promptly.

- Enhanced Accuracy:

AI systems are less prone to the kinds of errors humans can make, especially when dealing with large volumes of data. By automating the detection and response processes, AI reduces the likelihood of overlooking or misinterpreting critical data that could indicate a cybersecurity threat. This high level of accuracy is essential in an environment where even a small oversight can lead to significant security breaches.

- Consistency in Responses:

AI provides a consistent approach to cybersecurity. Unlike human operators, who may have varying levels of expertise and differing approaches, AI systems follow a set pattern of rules and behaviors. This consistency ensures that every incident is treated with the same level of scrutiny and according to the same protocols, reducing the risk of inconsistent handling of threats.

- Freeing Up Human Resources:

By taking over routine tasks, AI allows human cybersecurity professionals to focus on more complex and strategic aspects of cybersecurity. This not only optimizes the use of human skills but also improves job satisfaction as employees are engaged in more meaningful and challenging work.

- Learning and Adapting:

AI systems in cybersecurity are not static; they learn and adapt over time. By analyzing the outcomes of previous incidents and responses, these systems continuously refine and improve their algorithms. This means that the longer they are in operation, the more effective they become at identifying and responding to threats.

- Risk of Over-reliance on Automation:

While AI significantly reduces workload and errors, over-reliance on automated systems without adequate human oversight can be risky. It is important to maintain a balance where skilled cybersecurity professionals oversee and complement the AI's operations, stepping in for complex decision-making or when unusual situations arise that the AI might not be programmed to handle.

### › Integrated Response Mechanisms

Integrated response mechanisms in AI-driven cybersecurity refer to the coordination and collaboration between various AI tools and existing security systems. This integration ensures a cohesive and comprehensive approach to incident response.

In an integrated setup, AI systems do not operate in isolation. Instead, they interact with traditional security measures like firewalls, intrusion detection systems, antivirus software, and other network security tools. The integration allows these diverse systems to share information and insights, creating a more robust defense against cyber threats.

One of the key aspects of integrated response mechanisms is the use of APIs (Application Programming Interfaces) and standardized communication protocols. These enable different systems to communicate and work together effectively. For example, if an AI system detects an unusual pattern in network traffic, it can automatically alert the intrusion detection system to take a closer look, or it can instruct the firewall to block certain suspicious activities.

Another important element is the centralization of data and alerts. In many cybersecurity environments, data is collected from various sources. An integrated AI system can aggregate this data, analyze it comprehensively, and provide a unified view of the security posture. This centralization helps identify complex, multi-faceted threats that might be overlooked if the systems were operating separately.

Additionally, integrated response mechanisms often include a level of automation in decision-making processes. AI algorithms can make real-time decisions based on the data they receive from various sources. This rapid decision-making capability is crucial for responding to fast-moving threats like zero-day exploits or ransomware attacks.

Furthermore, integrated systems can adapt and evolve over time. They can learn from past incidents and responses, adjusting their algorithms and strategies for improved future performance. This adaptability is essential in a landscape where cyber threats are constantly evolving.

However, the challenge in integrated response mechanisms lies in ensuring compatibility and security among various components. There is a need for stringent security protocols to ensure that the integration itself does not become a vulnerability. Moreover, balancing automation with human oversight in integrated systems is crucial to handling unexpected scenarios or complex threats that require human intervention.

### › Real-time analytics and decision-making

Real-time analytics and decision-making are pivotal components of AI-driven cybersecurity systems. These systems utilize advanced algorithms to analyze vast amounts of data as it is generated, allowing for immediate identification of potential threats and rapid decision-making.

- Real-Time Data Analysis:

AI systems continuously monitor network traffic, user activities, and system logs, processing this data in real-time. This constant vigilance helps in detecting anomalies that could signify a security breach, such as unusual login attempts or unexpected data transfers. By analyzing patterns as, they emerge, AI can identify threats that might otherwise go unnoticed in the vast sea of data.

- Predictive Analytics:

Beyond just monitoring current activities, AI systems employ predictive analytics. They use historical data to predict future security incidents. This approach is based on the premise that many cyber-attacks follow recognizable patterns. By understanding these patterns, AI can anticipate attacks before they happen, allowing organizations to bolster defenses in vulnerable areas.

- Automated Decision-Making:

Once a potential threat is identified, AI systems are capable of making decisions on how to respond. These decisions are based on predefined criteria, such as the type of threat, its severity, and the potential impact on the organization. For instance, in response to detected malware, the AI system might automatically initiate a process to isolate the infected part of the network and start malware removal protocols.

- Enhanced Incident Response:

In traditional settings, human analysts would need to review alerts and decide on the course of action, which could take considerable time. With AI, this process is significantly faster, often happening in seconds. This rapid response is crucial in mitigating the impact of cyber-attacks.

- Integration with Other Systems:

Real-time analytics and decision-making capabilities are not isolated; they are often integrated with other security systems. For example, AI-driven decisions can trigger responses in firewalls, intrusion prevention systems, and data loss prevention tools, creating a coordinated defense mechanism.

- Continuous Learning and Adaptation:

AI systems in cybersecurity don't just respond to threats; they learn from them. Each incident provides new data points that help refine the algorithms, making them more accurate and effective over time. This continuous learning ensures that the systems adapt to evolving cyber threats.

- Challenges in Real-Time Analytics:

Despite the advantages, real-time analytics in cybersecurity faces challenges like false positives, where benign activities are wrongly identified as threats. Balancing sensitivity to detect actual threats without overwhelming the system with false alerts is a critical aspect of AI design in cybersecurity.

- Human Oversight:

While AI greatly enhances decision-making speed and efficiency, human oversight remains essential. Experts are needed to interpret complex situations, handle exceptions, and provide guidance on ethical and legal considerations.

# Chapter 5

# Case Studies: Ai In Action

# Real-World Examples of AI-Driven Incident Responses

### I.   Retail Giant Thwarts Phishing Attack

The AI Edge: The retail corporation's AI system was not just another spam filter. It was a sophisticated neural network trained on vast datasets of legitimate and phishing emails. By analyzing subtle patterns, like the writing style and the email metadata, the AI could detect phishing attempts that traditional software might miss.

Behind the Scenes: Once the suspicious email was identified, the AI system automatically cross-referenced it against known phishing databases and internally flagged patterns. It also used natural language processing to understand the content, looking for phishing red flags such as urgent calls to action or requests for sensitive information.

Impact on Business: The prompt detection and response saved the company from potential financial loss and reputational damage. It showcased AI's ability to provide proactive security measures far beyond the capabilities of traditional, reactive approaches.

### I.   Healthcare Provider Blocks Ransomware

Advanced Detection Techniques: The AI tool employed by the healthcare provider was not just monitoring for known ransomware signatures. It was analyzing behavior patterns – how files were being accessed and changed on the network. This behavioral analysis allowed it to spot ransomware-like activity even from previously unknown sources.

Response Protocol: Upon detecting suspicious activity, the AI system instantly moved to isolate the affected network segments, effectively quarantining the ransomware. This rapid response was crucial in preventing the spread of the ransomware to critical systems containing sensitive patient data.

Broader Implications: This incident highlighted the importance of AI in protecting sensitive health data, where traditional antivirus tools might not react swiftly enough to stop ransomware in its early stages.

## I. Financial Institution Detects Insider Threat

Contextual Awareness: The AI system in the bank was designed to understand normal user behavior patterns. When an employee started accessing an unusually large amount of sensitive data, the system detected this deviation from the norm.

Intelligent Response: The system didn't immediately block the employee's access, which could have been a false alarm. Instead, it started a more detailed analysis and alerted the cybersecurity team, allowing for a more nuanced response.

Preventing the Breach: By catching the insider threat early, the bank avoided a potential data breach that could have led to significant financial losses and erosion of customer trust. This case exemplified the necessity of AI in monitoring and analyzing user behavior to detect threats from within an organization.

## I. Technology Firm Mitigates DDoS Attack

Scenario: A leading technology firm faced a Distributed Denial of Service (DDoS) attack, aiming to overwhelm their servers with traffic.

AI-Driven Response: The firm's AI system, equipped with advanced network analysis tools, immediately detected the unusual surge in traffic. It differentiated malicious traffic from legitimate requests using pattern recognition and machine learning algorithms.

Outcome: The AI system dynamically rerouted traffic and filtered out malicious packets, mitigating the attack. This response minimized downtime and maintained service availability for legitimate users, showcasing the AI's ability to handle large-scale network threats.

## I.  E-commerce Platform Prevents Fraud

Scenario: An e-commerce platform was experiencing a spike in fraudulent transactions.

AI-Driven Response: Using AI-powered fraud detection algorithms, the platform analyzed transaction patterns in real time. The AI system looked for anomalies in purchasing behavior, geolocation discrepancies, and inconsistencies in payment methods.

Outcome: The AI system successfully identified and blocked fraudulent transactions, reducing financial losses and enhancing customer trust. This case illustrates AI's role in real-time analysis and decision-making in fraud prevention.

## I.  Manufacturing Company Addresses Supply Chain Vulnerability

Scenario: A global manufacturing company discovered vulnerabilities in its supply chain software, potentially exposing sensitive data.

AI-Driven Response: The company deployed an AI-driven security solution to monitor and analyze network traffic and user behavior across its supply chain network. The AI system used predictive analytics to identify potential security breaches before they could be exploited.

Outcome: The preemptive measures taken by the AI system prevented data breaches and ensured the integrity of the supply chain. This example highlights the importance of AI in protecting interconnected systems and networks.

## I.  University Thwarts Malware Spread

Scenario: A major university's network was targeted with sophisticated malware designed to steal research data.

AI-Driven Response: The university's AI-enabled cybersecurity system scanned for unusual data movements and access patterns across the network. Using heuristic analysis, the AI identified and isolated the malware-infected systems.

Outcome: The quick action by the AI system prevented the spread of malware and safeguarded critical academic research. This case underscores the value of AI in protecting educational institutions from advanced cyber threats.

*These examples highlight the transformative impact AI is having in the field of cybersecurity. AI-driven systems are not just faster; they bring a level of sophistication and proactive analysis that is changing the landscape of cyber incident response. Their ability to learn and adapt to new threats, coupled with their advanced detection capabilities, makes them invaluable assets in the ongoing battle against cyber threats.*

# Lessons Learned from AI Implementation

- Adaptability is Key: AI systems in cybersecurity need to constantly evolve. As cyber threats change and become more sophisticated, AI must be able to learn from these new patterns and adapt accordingly. It's not just about deploying an AI solution; it's about continuously training and updating it with the latest threat intelligence. This adaptability ensures that the AI remains effective over time, always staying a step ahead of potential cyber threats.

- Human-AI Collaboration: The synergy between AI and human expertise is crucial. AI greatly enhances the speed and efficiency of detecting and responding to incidents, but human oversight is essential for nuanced decision-making. Cybersecurity professionals bring a level of understanding and intuition that AI currently cannot replicate. This collaboration leads to a more robust and effective incident response strategy.

- Data Privacy Concerns: Implementing AI in cybersecurity must be done with a keen awareness of privacy issues. As these systems process large volumes of data, ensuring they comply with privacy laws and ethical standards is crucial. It's a delicate balance between using data to protect against threats and respecting individual privacy rights.

- Continuous Improvement: AI systems are not a one-time solution; they require ongoing attention and improvement. The cyber landscape is dynamic, and AI systems must be fed with the latest data and scenarios to stay effective. This continuous improvement is key to maintaining a strong defense against cyber threats.

- Tailored Solutions: Finally, AI implementations should be customized to fit the specific needs and context of the organization. Each organization has unique vulnerabilities and requires a tailored approach to cybersecurity. A generic AI solution might not address specific threats or integrate well with existing systems.

# Chapter 6

# Tools and Technologies In Ai-Driven Incident Response

In this chapter, we delve into the exciting world of tools and technologies that are at the forefront of AI-driven incident response. The focus is to provide you with an understanding of how these tools work and how they are revolutionizing the way we handle cybersecurity threats.

# Understanding AI-Driven Tools

In the realm of cybersecurity, AI-driven tools are like the high-tech guardians of the digital world. Their primary role is to protect networks, systems, and data from cyber threats, and they do this in ways that traditional tools can't match. Let's break down what makes these tools stand out:

AI at the Core: At the heart of these tools is Artificial Intelligence (AI). Unlike traditional software that follows strict, predefined rules, AI-driven tools are built to learn and adapt. They analyze data, learn from it, and make decisions based on their learning. The ability to learn and adapt is crucial in the ever-changing landscape of cybersecurity threats.

Real-Time Response: One of the biggest strengths of AI-driven tools is their ability to act fast. Cyber threats can strike at any moment, and the speed of response can be the difference between a minor hiccup and a major disaster. AI-driven tools can analyze and respond to threats in real time, often identifying and neutralizing threats before humans even become aware of them.

Predictive Capabilities: These tools don't just react to threats; they predict them. By analyzing patterns and trends in data, they can identify potential threats before they materialize. This predictive capability is a game-changer, shifting cybersecurity from a reactive to a proactive stance.

Customization and Learning: Every organization has unique cybersecurity needs. AI-driven tools can be customized for specific environments and continue to improve over time. They learn from the unique patterns and behaviors of their specific deployment environment, becoming more effective as they gather more data.

# Key Technologies Used in AI Tools

AI-driven cybersecurity tools aren't magic; they're powered by some groundbreaking technologies. Here's a look at the key tech under the hood:

i. Machine Learning (ML): ML is like the brain behind many AI tools. It learns from data to make smart predictions. In cybersecurity, ML can learn from past security problems to spot new ones.

ii. Deep Learning: Think of this as a part of ML that uses networks to study data. It's really good at finding patterns. So, it's great at catching tricky cyber threats.

iii. Natural Language Processing (NLP): This tech helps computers talk our language. In cybersecurity, NLP can look at how we talk online, find phishing emails, and even understand what cyber dangers are all about.

iv. Behavioral Analytics: By analyzing the behavior of users and systems, these tools can detect anomalies that might indicate a security breach. For instance, if a user suddenly accesses a large amount of data in an unusual pattern, it might signal a compromised account.

v. Automation and Orchestration: AI tools not only detect threats but also automate responses. Orchestration involves coordinating various security processes and tools. In an AI-driven system, once a threat is detected, responses can be automatically initiated, such as isolating affected systems or blocking malicious IPs.

# Types of AI-Driven Cybersecurity Tools

1. Intrusion Detection Systems (IDS): AI-driven IDS are advanced systems that monitor network traffic to identify potentially malicious activities. Unlike traditional IDS, AI-based systems can learn and adapt to new threats over time. They analyze patterns in data traffic and can distinguish between normal network behavior and anomalies that may signify a security breach.

2. Threat Intelligence Platforms: These platforms leverage AI to gather, analyze, and interpret large amounts of data from various sources about emerging or existing threats. They can process information from the dark web, forums, and other sources to provide real-time alerts about new vulnerabilities, malware, or attack strategies.

3. Automated Security Incident Response Systems: These systems use AI to automatically respond to detected threats. They can analyze the severity of an incident and decide on the best course of action, such as isolating affected systems, blocking suspicious IP addresses, or initiating countermeasures to prevent the spread of malware.

4. Behavioral Analytics Tools: By analyzing patterns of user behavior, these tools can detect anomalies that may indicate a security threat, such as unauthorized access or data exfiltration attempts. They use AI to understand baseline behaviors and flag activities that deviate from the norm.

5. Phishing Detection Tools: AI is used to identify phishing attempts more effectively than traditional spam filters. These tools analyze email content, sender information, and other attributes to detect sophisticated phishing tactics that might bypass standard detection

methods.

6. AI-Enabled Antivirus and Malware Detection: These tools utilize machine learning algorithms to detect and prevent malware, including variants that have not been seen before. They analyze the characteristics of files and programs to detect malicious intent, offering a more proactive approach than signature-based antivirus solutions.

7. Network Traffic Analysis Tools: AI-powered network traffic analysis tools provide comprehensive visibility into network activity. They can detect unusual data flows, unauthorized network accesses, or attempts to exfiltrate data, helping in the early detection of potential security incidents.

8. User and Entity Behavior Analytics (UEBA): These tools focus on detecting insider threats and compromised accounts. They analyze user behavior and compare it to established patterns to identify risky activities that might indicate a security threat from within the organization.

9. Security Orchestration, Automation, and Response (SOAR) Tools: SOAR tools combine AI with automation to manage and respond to security alerts. They can prioritize alerts based on severity, automate responses to low-level threats, and provide security teams with tools for more efficient incident management.

10. Vulnerability Management Tools: These tools use AI to scan systems and applications for vulnerabilities. They prioritize vulnerabilities based on potential impact and the likelihood of exploitation, helping organizations focus their remediation efforts where they are most needed.

Each of these AI-driven tools plays a crucial role in the modern cybersecurity landscape, offering enhanced capabilities to prevent, predict, detect, and respond to cyber threats more effectively than ever before. Their integration into cybersecurity strategies represents a significant advancement in protecting digital assets and information in an increasingly interconnected world.

# Benefits of AI-Driven Tools in Incident Response

AI-driven tools bring a transformative approach to incident response in cybersecurity. The benefits they offer are substantial and diverse:

- Speed: The speed with which these tools operate is one of their most significant advantages. AI systems can process and analyze data at a much faster rate than humans. This rapid processing allows for quicker detection of threats and faster responses to incidents, which is crucial in minimizing damage.

- Accuracy: AI-driven tools are designed to be highly accurate in detecting cybersecurity threats. By learning from vast datasets, these tools can identify subtle patterns and anomalies that might be overlooked by human analysts. This precision helps in reducing false positives (incorrect threat alerts) and false negatives (missed threats), leading to more reliable security measures.

- Adaptability: AI systems can learn and adapt over time. As they are exposed to new data and scenarios, their ability to detect and respond to threats improves. This means that AI-driven tools can become more effective as they are used, staying up-to-date with the latest types of cyber threats.

- Proactive Threat Management: Unlike traditional tools that often react to threats after they occur, AI-driven tools can predict and prevent incidents. By analyzing trends and patterns, they can identify potential threats before they materialize, allowing for proactive measures to be taken.

- Resource Efficiency: AI tools automate many aspects of incident detection and response, which can significantly reduce the workload on human security teams. This allows cybersecurity professionals to focus on more complex tasks and strategic planning, improving overall efficiency.

- Comprehensive Coverage: AI-driven tools can monitor and analyze data from a vast array of sources simultaneously. This comprehensive coverage ensures that no part of the system is left unchecked, enhancing overall security posture.

# Challenges and Considerations

Despite their numerous benefits, AI-driven tools in incident response also present certain challenges and considerations:

- Data Dependency: AI systems rely heavily on data to learn and make decisions. The quality and quantity of data available significantly impact their effectiveness. Inaccurate data can lead to incorrect conclusions, making the system less reliable.

- Complexity and Expertise: Implementing and managing AI-driven tools requires a certain level of expertise. Understanding how these systems work, interpreting their outputs, and integrating them into existing security infrastructures can be complex tasks.

- Ethical and Privacy Concerns: The use of AI in cybersecurity raises important questions about privacy and ethical use of data. Ensuring that these tools comply with legal standards and ethical guidelines is crucial, especially when dealing with sensitive personal or organizational data.

- Evolving Threats: Cyber threats are constantly evolving, and there is always a risk that AI-driven tools might not keep pace with new types of attacks. AI models must be updated and trained on a regular basis to ensure their effectiveness against emerging threats.

- Dependence and Overreliance: There is a risk of becoming overly dependent on AI tools, potentially leading to a lack of human oversight. It's important to maintain a balance between automated and manual processes in cybersecurity.

- Integration Challenges: Effectively integrating AI tools with existing cybersecurity systems and protocols can be challenging. Ensuring compatibility and seamless operation is crucial for the effective deployment of these tools.

# Integrating AI Tools into Existing Security Infrastructures

Integrating AI tools into your current security infrastructure is a critical step in enhancing your cybersecurity capabilities. This process involves several important considerations and actions:

1. Assessment of Current Security Posture: Begin by evaluating your existing security infrastructure. Understand the strengths and weaknesses, and identify areas where AI can bring improvements. This might include areas like threat detection, incident response, or predictive analytics.

2. Selecting Appropriate AI Tools: Once you know where your security posture can benefit from AI, the next step is to choose the right tools. Look for solutions that are not only powerful in terms of AI capabilities but also compatible with your existing systems. Consider factors like ease of integration, scalability, and support from the vendor.

3. Planning for Integration: Integration of AI tools should be planned meticulously. This involves mapping out how these tools will interact with your existing systems, what data they will access, and how they will communicate with other security solutions. Ensure that the integration doesn't disrupt existing security operations.

4. Training and Skill Development: One of the key aspects of successful integration is ensuring your team has the necessary skills. Invest in training for your IT and security teams so they can effectively manage

and leverage the new AI tools. This training should cover not just technical aspects but also ethical considerations in using AI.

5. Testing and Deployment: Before fully deploying AI tools, conduct thorough testing. This could include pilot programs or running the AI tools in a controlled environment to see how they interact with your existing setup. Pay attention to any compatibility issues or unexpected behaviors.

6. Continuous Monitoring and Adjustment: After deployment, continuously monitor the performance of the AI tools. Be prepared to make adjustments, whether it's fine-tuning the AI algorithms or addressing integration issues. AI tools often require ongoing training and updating to stay effective.

7. Compliance and Security: Ensure that the integration of AI tools complies with relevant laws and regulations, especially those related to data privacy and security. The use of AI should enhance your security posture without compromising legal and ethical standards.

# Looking Ahead

The future of AI in cybersecurity is promising and continually evolving. Looking ahead, several trends and developments are likely to shape how AI tools are integrated into security infrastructures:

1. Advancements in AI and Machine Learning: AI and machine learning technologies are rapidly advancing, offering more sophisticated and efficient ways to handle cybersecurity. Expect to see AI becoming more adept at predictive analytics, identifying threats even before they manifest.

2. Increased Automation in Security Processes: The trend is towards more automation in security processes, reducing the need for human intervention and allowing for quicker responses to incidents.

3. Rising Importance of Ethical AI: As AI becomes more integral to cybersecurity, the focus on ethical AI will intensify. This includes ensuring privacy, fairness, and transparency in how AI systems operate and make decisions.

4. Integration with Cloud and IoT: With the rise of cloud computing and the Internet of Things (IoT), AI tools will increasingly need to be integrated with these technologies, addressing the unique security challenges they bring.

5. Challenges and Opportunities with Big Data: The vast amount of data generated by modern technologies provides both a challenge and an opportunity for AI in cybersecurity. Efficiently processing and leveraging this data for security purposes will be a key focus area.

6. Collaborative AI Solutions: Expect a rise in collaborative efforts, both in terms of technology sharing between AI systems and in partnerships between organizations, to strengthen cybersecurity

defenses.

# Chapter 7

# Building an Ai-Driven
# Incident Response Team

# Introduction

In today's fast-evolving cybersecurity landscape, the need for an AI-driven incident response team is more critical than ever. But what does it take to build such a team? This chapter will guide you through the essential steps and considerations.

## Skills and Roles Required for an AI-Driven Incident Response Team

Building an AI-driven incident response team involves assembling a group of professionals with diverse but complementary skills. Let's delve into the specific roles and the skills required for each to handle cybersecurity incidents using AI technology effectively.

### 1. Cybersecurity Analysts/Experts

Skills Needed:

- Deep understanding of cybersecurity principles, practices, and tools.
- Ability to identify and assess cybersecurity threats and vulnerabilities.
- Experience in incident detection, analysis, and response.
- Knowledge of regulatory compliance and security frameworks.

Role in the Team:

- Lead in identifying and mitigating cyber threats.
- Coordinate the incident response process.
- Guide the integration of AI tools into cybersecurity practices.

## 2. AI and Machine Learning Specialists

<u>Skills Needed:</u>

- Expertise in AI and machine learning algorithms and technologies.
- Proficiency in programming languages like Python, R, or Java.
- Experience in developing, training, and deploying AI models.
- Skills in data analysis and pattern recognition.

<u>Role in the Team:</u>

- Develop and fine-tune AI algorithms for threat detection and response.
- Collaborate with cybersecurity experts to align AI tools with security needs.
- Continuously update AI models to adapt to new threats.

## 3. Data Analysts/Scientists

<u>Skills Needed:</u>

- Strong analytical skills with the ability to interpret complex data sets.
- Proficiency in data analytics tools and software.
- Understanding of data management and governance.
- Skills in statistical analysis and reporting.

<u>Role in the Team:</u>

- Analyze security data to identify trends and patterns.
- Provide insights to inform AI model training and cybersecurity strategies.
- Ensure data integrity and compliance.

## 4. IT and Network Professionals

<u>Skills Needed:</u>

- Knowledge of IT infrastructure, network architecture, and system administration.

- Experience with cloud computing and virtualization technologies.
- Skills in troubleshooting and maintaining network security.
- Understanding of the integration of AI tools into IT environments.

Role in the Team:

- Manage and secure the IT infrastructure.
- Implement and maintain AI cybersecurity tools.
- Ensure seamless integration of AI solutions with existing systems.

## 5. Incident Response Coordinator
Skills Needed:

- Strong organizational and leadership abilities.
- Excellent communication and coordination skills.
- Experience in project management and process coordination.
- Understanding of incident response protocols and procedures.

Role in the Team:

- Oversee the incident response process.
- Ensure effective communication within the team and with external stakeholders.
- Coordinate training and development activities.

## 6. Legal and Compliance Advisor
Skills Needed:

- Knowledge of legal aspects related to cybersecurity and data privacy.
- Understanding of compliance requirements and standards.
- Skills in risk assessment and management.

Role in the Team:

- Advise on legal and ethical considerations in AI implementation.
- Ensure compliance with data protection laws and regulations.

- Manage legal aspects of incident responses.

# Training and Developing AI Competency

In the realm of AI-driven cybersecurity, training and developing AI competency is a dynamic and ongoing process. It involves equipping your team with the necessary skills and knowledge to integrate AI into your incident response strategy effectively. Let's delve into how you can achieve this.

- Understanding the Basics of AI and Machine Learning

Start with the basics. Ensure that your team members, especially those from non-AI backgrounds, have a fundamental understanding of AI and machine learning concepts. This could include how AI algorithms work, the basics of neural networks, and understanding machine learning models.

- Specialized AI Training for Cybersecurity

AI in cybersecurity is a specialized field. Offer training sessions focused on how AI can be used in threat detection, anomaly detection, and predictive analytics. This might involve understanding how AI can identify patterns in large datasets that indicate a security threat.

- Hands-on Workshops and Simulations

Practical experience is key. Conduct workshops where your team can work with real data and AI tools. Simulations of cybersecurity incidents using AI can provide invaluable practical experience and help your team understand the nuances of AI-driven responses.

- Collaborative Learning Environments

Encourage a collaborative learning environment where AI specialists and cybersecurity professionals can share knowledge. This cross-pollination of ideas and skills is crucial for developing a well-rounded AI competency.

- Continuous Learning and Up-to-Date Knowledge

The field of AI is constantly evolving. Ensure that your team has access to the latest research, tools, and techniques in AI and cybersecurity. This can be through subscriptions to leading journals, attending webinars, and participating in relevant online forums and communities.

- Ethics and Bias Training

Given the ethical implications of AI, it's crucial to include training on ethical AI use. Teach your team about the importance of data privacy, the risks of biased algorithms, and how to develop AI solutions that are fair and unbiased.

- Vendor-Specific Training

If you are using specific AI tools or platforms, consider vendor-specific training. Many AI technology providers offer detailed training programs for their products which can be highly beneficial.

- Mentorship and Expert Guidance

Mentorship can play a significant role in developing AI competency. Pairing less experienced team members with AI experts can facilitate a more personalized learning experience. Also, consider bringing in external experts for seminars or workshops.

- Certifications and Advanced Courses

Encourage your team to pursue certifications or advanced courses in AI and cybersecurity. This not only boosts their skills but also keeps them engaged and motivated.

- Feedback and Continuous Improvement

Finally, regularly solicit feedback from your team on their training needs. This will help you tailor future training initiatives and ensure that your team's AI competency continuously improves to meet the evolving demands of cybersecurity.

# Chapter 8

# Legal and Ethical Considerations

In this chapter, we dive into the important legal and ethical aspects of using AI in cybersecurity. It's crucial to understand that while AI offers great benefits, it also brings challenges and responsibilities, especially when handling sensitive data and making automated decisions.

### 1. Privacy Concerns in AI-Driven Cybersecurity

When we talk about AI in cybersecurity, one of the most critical issues that emerge is privacy. The use of AI often involves processing large amounts of data, some of which can be highly sensitive. This raises several privacy concerns that need careful consideration.

- The Nature of Data in Cybersecurity AI

In cybersecurity, AI systems are typically trained with vast amounts of data, including personal user information, to detect and respond to threats effectively. This data can range from simple log files to more personal data like emails, browsing histories, or even biometric data. The sensitive nature of this data means there's a high risk involved if it's mishandled.

- Data Collection and Consent

A key privacy concern is how this data is collected. Users are often unaware of what data is being collected and how it's being used. Transparency is crucial here. Users should be informed, and, where possible, their consent should be obtained. This not only builds trust but also aligns with legal standards in many regions.

- Data Storage and Access

Once collected, how data is stored and who has access to it is another significant concern. Ensuring that data is stored securely and that access is limited to authorized personnel is fundamental. Encryption and other security measures are vital to protect this data from unauthorized access, including potential internal threats.

- Uses of Data in AI Models

The way data is used in training and operating AI models also raises privacy issues. There's a risk that AI systems might inadvertently expose personal data, especially if they are not designed with privacy in mind. Techniques like anonymization and pseudonymization can help reduce this risk by removing or altering personal identifiers in data.

- Compliance with Privacy Laws

Globally, there are various laws and regulations, like the GDPR in Europe and the CCPA in California, which set standards for data privacy and security. These laws often require organizations to implement specific measures to protect personal data and to report breaches. Compliance with these regulations is not just a legal obligation but also a matter of ethical responsibility.

- Balancing Security and Privacy

Finally, a delicate balance must be maintained between using AI for effective cybersecurity and respecting user privacy. This balance requires a thoughtful approach to how AI systems are designed and deployed. It involves making strategic decisions about what data is necessary for security purposes and how to process and store that data responsibly.

1.  **Ethical AI Use in Cybersecurity**

In the rapidly evolving world of AI-driven cybersecurity, the ethical use of artificial intelligence is not just a secondary concern but a fundamental necessity. As AI systems increasingly automate the detection and response to cyber threats, we must consider the ethical implications of these technologies.

- Understanding the Ethical Landscape of AI in Cybersecurity

At its core, ethical AI use in cybersecurity revolves around creating systems that are not only effective but also fair, transparent, and accountable. As these systems process vast amounts of data, including potentially sensitive personal information, the ethical handling of this data becomes paramount. This involves ensuring that AI systems respect privacy rights and adhere to data protection laws, which are designed to safeguard individual information.

- The Challenge of Bias and Fairness

One of the most pressing ethical concerns in Artificial Intelligence is the issue of bias. AI systems learn from data, and if this data contains biases, the AI's decisions and actions might also be biased. In cybersecurity, this could mean unfairly targeting certain groups or failing to protect others. Addressing these biases requires consciously using diverse and representative datasets and, continuously monitoring AI systems for biased outcomes, and adjusting them as needed.

- Transparency in AI Decision-Making

Transparency is another critical aspect of ethical AI. In the context of cybersecurity, this means that when an AI system identifies a threat or makes a security decision, the process behind this decision should be understandable to human operators. This transparency is crucial not only for trust but also for accountability. When security incidents occur, it's important to be able to trace back the AI's decision-making process to understand what happened and why.

- Accountability and Responsibility

With AI systems playing a crucial role in cybersecurity, questions of accountability arise. Who is responsible if an AI system fails to detect a significant threat or mistakenly identifies benign activities as threats, who is responsible? The ethical use of AI in cybersecurity demands clear guidelines on accountability. This includes establishing who is responsible for the AI's actions - the developers, the users, or the AI itself? It also involves ensuring that there are processes in place for correcting mistakes and learning from them.

- Ethical Development and Deployment

Ethical AI use extends beyond just the operational phase; it starts right from the development stage. Ethical AI development in cybersecurity means considering the potential impacts of AI systems on all stakeholders, including users, targets of cybersecurity measures, and society at large. It also involves involving diverse perspectives in the development process to anticipate and mitigate ethical risks.

## 1. Navigating Legal Frameworks

In the world of AI-driven cybersecurity, navigating legal frameworks is a complex but essential task. As AI technologies rapidly evolve, legal systems around the world are striving to keep pace, resulting in a mosaic of regulations that any organization employing AI must carefully consider.

The legal landscape of AI in cybersecurity is influenced by a variety of factors including data protection laws, international cybersecurity standards, and specific regulations governing AI's use. For instance, in the European Union, the General Data Protection Regulation (GDPR) has set a precedent for handling personal data, impacting how AI systems can be used for processing and analyzing such data. In contrast, countries like the United States have a more decentralized approach, with sector-specific regulations and state-level laws.

One of the key challenges in navigating these legal frameworks is their dynamic nature. Laws and regulations are continuously updated to address new cybersecurity threats and the evolving capabilities of AI. This requires organizations to stay informed and agile, adapting their AI strategies in response to legal changes. It's not just about compliance; it's about understanding how these laws reflect broader concerns about privacy, security, and ethical use of technology.

Moreover, the international scope of cybersecurity and AI adds another layer of complexity. Cyber threats don't respect national borders, and AI-driven solutions often involve cross-border data flows and collaborations. This global aspect necessitates an understanding of not only domestic laws but also international regulations and treaties. For businesses operating in multiple countries, this means crafting AI strategies that are flexible enough to comply with diverse legal requirements.

Legal implications also extend to liability issues. In cases where AI-driven security systems fail or are breached, determining liability can be challenging. Who is responsible when an AI system makes a mistake or is manipulated? Is it the developer of the AI, the user, or the entity that provided the training data? These questions are still being debated in legal circles, and the answers may vary depending on the jurisdiction and specific circumstances.

To navigate this complex legal framework effectively, organizations must adopt a proactive approach. This includes engaging with legal experts specializing in cybersecurity and AI, staying abreast of legal developments, and integrating legal considerations into the AI development and deployment process. It also involves active participation in policy discussions and standard-setting initiatives to help shape a legal environment that supports innovation while protecting against cyber threats and respecting ethical norms.

# Ethical Decision-Making in AI Development

Ethical decision-making in AI development, especially in the realm of cybersecurity, is a critical and multifaceted process. It demands a diligent approach to how AI systems are designed, developed, and deployed. This focus ensures that the AI not only performs its intended function effectively but also aligns with broader societal values and ethical principles.

- Integrating Ethics from the Ground Up

Ethical considerations must be integrated into the AI development process from the very beginning. This means that ethics are not an afterthought but a fundamental part of the design and planning phases. Developers and project managers should ask key questions: What are the potential impacts of this AI system on individuals and society? Could the system inadvertently harm or disadvantage certain groups of people? These questions guide the development towards more responsible and equitable outcomes.

- Diverse Teams for Diverse Perspectives

One of the most effective ways to ensure ethical development is to involve a diverse range of perspectives in the AI creation process. This diversity isn't limited to professional background or expertise but includes factors like cultural, gender, and socioeconomic diversity. Such a team is more likely to identify potential biases or ethical blind spots in AI systems, leading to more inclusive and fair AI solutions.

- Addressing Bias Proactively

AI systems, particularly those in cybersecurity, often rely on large datasets for training. These datasets can contain biases, which the AI might then learn and perpetuate. Ethical AI development involves actively searching for and mitigating these biases. This might include carefully curating datasets, using techniques to balance data, or designing robust algorithms against biased data inputs.

- Transparency and Explainability

Another cornerstone of ethical AI is transparency. This means making the AI's decision-making processes as clear and understandable as possible. In cybersecurity, where AI might be making crucial decisions about threat detection or data privacy, stakeholders need to understand how and why certain decisions are made. This transparency builds trust and facilitates more effective oversight and accountability.

- Ethical Testing and Deployment

Testing AI systems for ethical integrity is just as important as testing them for functional performance. This involves rigorous evaluation to ensure the AI behaves as intended in various scenarios, including edge cases. Deployment should be cautiously approached with continuous monitoring to identify and correct any ethical issues that arise post-deployment quickly.

- Adapting to Evolving Ethical Standards

The field of AI and the societal understanding of ethics are both evolving rapidly. What is considered ethical today might change in the future. Therefore, ethical AI development is an ongoing process. Developers and organizations must stay informed about the latest discussions and developments in AI ethics and be prepared to adapt their systems and practices accordingly.

# Chapter 9

# The Future of AI In Cybersecurity

# Emerging Trends and Technologies

As we look toward the future of AI in cybersecurity, several emerging trends and technologies stand out as game-changers. These advancements are not just reshaping how we approach security but also how we think about the relationship between artificial intelligence and digital protection.

1. Predictive Analytics and AI's Anticipatory Nature: One of the most groundbreaking developments in AI for cybersecurity is the shift toward predictive analytics. Traditional security measures often focus on mitigating threats as they occur, but predictive analytics changes this reactive stance to a proactive one. AI systems can now analyze numerous datasets to identify potential vulnerabilities and patterns that could indicate a future threat. This predictive capability allows organizations to strengthen their defenses before an attack occurs, significantly reducing the risk of damage.

2. The Rise of Self-Learning Systems: Another significant trend is the development of self-learning systems in cybersecurity. These systems utilize machine learning algorithms to improve their detection and response capabilities continuously. Unlike traditional systems that require manual updates and rule-setting, self-learning systems adapt autonomously to new threats. This continuous learning process ensures that security systems remain up-to-date and effective against even the most novel cyber threats.

3. Automated Response Mechanisms: The future of AI in cybersecurity also lies in the ability of systems to not only detect threats but to respond to them autonomously. This automation of response actions

means dramatically reducing the time taken to react to a security breach. Automated responses can include a range of actions, from isolating compromised systems to implementing pre-planned countermeasures. This rapid response capability is crucial in minimizing the impact of cyber-attacks.

4. Advancements in Threat Intelligence: AI is transforming threat intelligence by integrating and analyzing information from many sources. This integrated approach provides this comprehensive understanding of the cybersecurity landscape. AI-driven threat intelligence can identify trends, anticipate new types of attacks, and offer insights into the most effective defense strategies. This intelligence is not just about gathering data; it's about making sense of it in a way that can be strategically applied.

5. AI and the Internet of Things (IoT): With the exponential growth of IoT devices, securing these interconnected systems has become a paramount concern. AI is at the forefront of safeguarding the IoT ecosystem. By continuously monitoring these devices, AI can detect anomalies that may indicate a security breach. The challenge here is immense due to the diversity and number of devices involved, but AI's scalability makes it uniquely suited for this task.

6. Combating AI-Enhanced Cyber Threats: As cybersecurity tools evolve, so do the tactics of cybercriminals. We are now seeing the emergence of AI-enhanced cyber threats. These threats use AI to learn from defensive measures and adapt to circumvent them. The cybersecurity field is essentially engaged in an arms race with hackers, where both parties are leveraging AI to outmaneuver the other. These dynamic underscores the need for continuous innovation in AI-driven cybersecurity measures.

7. Ethical AI Development and Trust: As AI takes on a more central role in cybersecurity, questions around ethics and trust come to the forefront. Ensuring that AI systems are developed with ethical considerations and are free from biases is crucial. Trust in AI systems is essential, not just for their effectiveness but also for their widespread adoption.

# Predictions and Preparations
## for Future Threats

As we delve into the future of AI in cybersecurity, it's crucial to recognize that the digital landscape is rapidly evolving, bringing with it a new era of threats and challenges. The increasing sophistication of cyber-attacks, propelled by technological advancements, requires a forward-thinking approach to ensure robust defense mechanisms. The adoption and integration of AI in cybersecurity strategies are pivotal in this ongoing battle against cyber threats. However, with these advancements come the necessity for predictions and preparations to stay one step ahead of potential risks.

The future of cybersecurity is inextricably linked to the development and deployment of AI. As AI systems become more advanced, they will not only identify and mitigate threats but also predict them before they materialize. This predictive capability is a double-edged sword; while it offers enhanced security, it also demands cybersecurity professionals' deeper understanding and vigilance. Cybercriminals are increasingly leveraging AI to develop more sophisticated attack methods. This evolving landscape suggests a future where the line between defender and attacker blurs, with both using advanced AI tools.

One of the critical aspects of preparing for future threats is the continuous evolution of AI algorithms. These algorithms must be trained on up-to-date data, ensuring they can recognize and respond to the latest types of cyber-attacks. This requires not only technological investments but also a commitment to ongoing research and development. As AI systems learn and adapt, they must do so in a way that prioritizes security and privacy, ensuring that they are not inadvertently creating new vulnerabilities.

Another vital area of focus is the human element in cybersecurity. While AI can handle an increasing number of tasks, the role of skilled cybersecurity professionals remains crucial. These professionals must understand the intricacies of AI systems and the ever-changing nature of cyber threats. Continuous education and training will be essential, ensuring that the human operators behind these systems can effectively oversee AI operations and intervene when necessary.

The integration of AI in cybersecurity also calls for robust ethical frameworks. As AI systems make more decisions, the need for transparent, fair, and unbiased algorithms becomes paramount. Ensuring that AI systems adhere to ethical guidelines and do not infringe on individual privacy rights is crucial. This includes developing and enforcing regulations that govern the use of AI in cybersecurity, ensuring that these powerful tools are used responsibly.

In addition to technological and ethical considerations, there is a need for global collaboration in the cybersecurity arena. Sharing knowledge, threat intelligence, and best practices among organizations, countries, and individuals will be vital in combating future cyber threats. This collaborative approach can lead to more effective strategies, quicker responses to new threats, and a more comprehensive understanding of the global cybersecurity landscape.

Preparing for future threats also involves recognizing the importance of resilience. As cyber threats evolve, expecting that all attacks can be prevented is unrealistic. Therefore, organizations must focus on developing robust recovery and response plans. This includes regular backups, incident response protocols, and business continuity plans. Building resilience into cybersecurity strategies ensures that even when attacks occur, the impact is minimized, and recovery is swift.

# Chapter 10

# Implementing AI-Driven Incident Response

# Steps to Transition to an AI-Driven Approach

Transitioning to an AI-driven approach in incident response is a strategic endeavor that requires a thoughtful and systematic approach. This chapter outlines the key steps organizations should undertake to successfully integrate AI into their cybersecurity operations, ensuring enhanced efficiency and effectiveness in handling cyber threats.

- <u>Understanding the Current Incident Response Framework</u>

The first step is to gain a deep understanding of the existing incident response framework. This involves evaluating the current procedures, tools, and capabilities of the cybersecurity team. Identifying gaps and areas where AI can add value is essential. For instance, AI might be particularly useful in automating the detection of anomalies or streamlining the analysis of large volumes of data.

- <u>Setting Clear, Strategic Objectives for AI Integration</u>

It is crucial to define what you aim to achieve with AI. Goals should be specific, measurable, achievable, relevant, and time-bound (SMART). These objectives could range from reducing response times to improving threat detection accuracy. Prioritizing these objectives helps in focusing efforts and resources effectively.

- <u>Selecting Appropriate AI Tools and Solutions</u>

Choosing the right AI tools and technologies is a critical step. This requires researching the market to understand the available options, assessing their effectiveness, and ensuring their compatibility with existing systems. The selected AI solutions should not only address the current needs but also be scalable and adaptable for future requirements.

- <u>Enhancing Team Capabilities to Work with AI</u>

For a successful AI implementation, the incident response team must possess the necessary skills and knowledge. This might involve training existing staff on AI basics and its applications in cybersecurity or hiring new talent with specialized AI expertise. The team must understand the technical aspects and the ethical and legal implications of using AI in cybersecurity.

- <u>Developing a Phased Integration Plan</u>

Implementing AI should be a gradual process. Start with pilot projects or small-scale implementations to test the effectiveness of AI tools. This approach allows for fine-tuning and adjustments before a full-scale roll-out. The integration plan should include clear milestones and metrics for success.

- <u>Testing and Validating the AI Implementation</u>

Before relying fully on AI-driven processes, it's important to test and validate them rigorously. This could involve conducting simulation drills and scenario-based exercises to evaluate the AI system's performance. Feedback from these tests is crucial for refining and optimizing the AI implementation.

- <u>Ensuring Continuous Monitoring and Optimization</u>

Once AI tools are integrated, continuous monitoring of their performance is vital. Establishing key performance indicators helps in assessing their impact and effectiveness. Regular updates and adjustments are necessary to ensure the AI models remain relevant and effective in the ever-evolving landscape of cybersecurity threats.

- <u>Creating a Culture of Innovation and Continuous Learning</u>

To fully leverage AI, organizations must foster a culture of innovation and continuous learning. Encourage team members to stay up to date on the latest AI advancements and cybersecurity trends. Promoting open communication and knowledge sharing helps in nurturing an environment where innovative ideas can thrive.

- <u>Adhering to Compliance and Ethical Standards</u>

As AI is integrated into cybersecurity processes, ensuring compliance with legal and regulatory requirements is imperative. Developing ethical guidelines for AI use is equally important. This ensures responsible and transparent use of AI, maintaining trust and integrity in the organization's cybersecurity practices.

- <u>Review and Refinement: An Ongoing Process</u>

Finally, the process of implementing AI in incident response should be viewed as iterative and ongoing. Regular reviews and assessments are necessary to determine if the AI-driven approach meets the set objectives and delivers value. Insights gained from these reviews should be used for continuous improvement and adaptation of the AI strategy.

*By following these steps, organizations can effectively transition to an AI-driven incident response system. This transition not only enhances their ability to respond to cybersecurity threats but also positions them to adapt to future challenges in the digital landscape.*

# Best Practices and Strategies for Implementing AI-Driven Incident Response

Implementing AI in incident response requires a careful blend of technical acumen, strategic foresight, and ethical considerations. Here's a comprehensive guide on how to navigate this transition:

- Ensuring High-Quality Data

The foundation of any effective AI system is high-quality data. This means not only gathering data from a wide range of sources but also ensuring its accuracy and relevance to the types of cyber threats your organization faces. Regular data audits are crucial to maintain the integrity of the data. These audits should assess the accuracy, remove any outdated information, and continuously update the dataset to reflect the evolving nature of cyber threats.

- Balancing Automation with Human Judgment

AI excels at handling high-volume, repetitive tasks, but human insight remains irreplaceable, especially for complex decision-making processes. It's important to establish clear boundaries: let AI handle the rapid, initial analysis of incidents, but reserve the more nuanced judgments and decisions for your human team. Moreover, continuous training of both the AI system and the human team is essential. The AI needs to be trained with updated scenarios and data, while the team must be skilled in interpreting AI findings and making informed decisions.

- Fostering Continuous Learning and Adaptation

A culture of continuous learning and experimentation is vital. Encouraging your team to try new methods, tools, and strategies keeps your organization at the forefront of cybersecurity advancements. Additionally, staying abreast of the latest trends and developments in AI and cybersecurity is necessary. This could involve participating in industry seminars, engaging in professional forums, or subscribing to leading cybersecurity publications.

- Upholding Compliance and Ethical Standards

As you integrate AI into your cybersecurity processes, it's crucial to navigate the legal and ethical landscape carefully. This includes ensuring that your AI practices comply with all relevant laws and regulations, particularly those concerning data privacy and protection. Equally important is the adherence to ethical standards. Develop a set of ethical guidelines for AI usage in your organization, particularly regarding data handling and privacy concerns.

- Collaboration and Knowledge Sharing

Cybersecurity, especially in the realm of AI, benefits greatly from collaboration and knowledge sharing. Engaging with other organizations, participating in industry forums, and sharing experiences and insights can lead to more robust and effective cybersecurity strategies. This collaborative approach not only enhances your own organization's defenses but also contributes to the broader community's understanding and preparedness against cyber threats.

- Embracing Organizational Change

Implementing AI in incident response will inevitably bring about changes in workflows and possibly in team structures. Preparing your team for these changes is crucial. This preparation involves training, clear communication, and creating an environment that is receptive to change. Being agile and open to adapting your strategies based on feedback and new insights is also key.

- Developing and Integrating Tailored AI Strategies

Customizing AI solutions to fit your specific needs is far more effective than adopting a generic approach. This customization involves understanding the unique threats your organization faces and tailoring your AI tools accordingly. Furthermore, these AI tools should seamlessly integrate with your existing security infrastructure, facilitating a unified and effective defense mechanism.

- Regular Monitoring and Reviews

Once your AI-driven incident response system is in place, continuous monitoring is essential. This includes keeping an eye out for any anomalies or unexpected behaviors from the AI systems. In addition to regular monitoring, periodic reviews should be scheduled to assess the effectiveness and efficiency of the AI strategies. These reviews should inform necessary updates and adjustments to AI models and algorithms, ensuring they remain effective against evolving cyber threats.

# Conclusion

# Summarizing the AI Revolution in Incident Handling

The journey through the AI revolution in incident handling is a story of significant advancement and change. AI has redefined the landscape of cybersecurity, turning what was once a reactive process into a proactive and dynamic system.

At the heart of this transformation is the capability of AI to analyze numerous amounts of data at unprecedented speeds. Traditional methods relied heavily on manual input and often lagged in identifying new threats. AI, on the other hand, brings a level of speed and precision that was previously unattainable. It can sift through data, identify patterns, and flag anomalies in real time. This means that potential threats are detected much faster, often before they can cause any harm.

Another crucial aspect of AI in incident handling is its learning ability. Machine learning algorithms, a subset of AI, can learn from past incidents, continuously improving their ability to detect and respond to new threats. This ongoing learning process means that AI-driven systems become more effective over time, adapting to the ever-evolving landscape of cyber threats.

AI has also democratized cybersecurity to some extent. Smaller organizations, which previously might not have had the resources for extensive cybersecurity teams, can now leverage AI tools to enhance their security. These tools can perform tasks that would require significant human labor, such as monitoring network traffic, scanning for vulnerabilities, and even responding to certain types of incidents automatically.

Furthermore, AI has paved the way for advanced threat intelligence. By aggregating and analyzing data from multiple sources, AI systems can provide insights into global threat trends, helping organizations stay ahead of potential risks. This global perspective is crucial in a world where cyber threats know no borders.

However, the AI revolution in incident handling is not just about technology; it's also about people. The role of the cybersecurity professional is evolving. Instead of being replaced by AI, these professionals are needed to guide, interpret, and make strategic decisions based on AI's findings. The human element remains critical, as ethical considerations, context understanding, and strategic planning are areas where AI cannot fully operate independently.

In summary, the AI revolution in incident handling marks a new era in cybersecurity. It brings speed, efficiency, learning capabilities, and global intelligence to the forefront. As we move forward, the synergy between human expertise and AI will define the future of cybersecurity, making it more resilient, responsive, and adaptive to emerging threats.

## Future Prospects and Final Thoughts

In the future landscape of AI-driven cybersecurity, we anticipate a transformation marked by advancements and challenges. AI is poised to extend its capabilities far beyond current limits, evolving into a tool that not only identifies and responds to threats but also predicts them. This shift towards predictive security could redefine how organizations approach cyber threats, enabling them to preemptively counter risks before they fully emerge.

The synergy between AI systems and human cybersecurity experts is expected to deepen, creating a powerful combination of computational efficiency and human insight. This collaboration will be crucial in developing nuanced and highly effective cybersecurity strategies.

AI's protective reach is likely to expand to cover emerging technologies such as the Internet of Things (IoT), autonomous vehicles, and smart city infrastructures. This expansion requires AI systems to continuously adapt and learn, ensuring robust security in an increasingly interconnected world.

However, the growth of AI in cybersecurity also brings significant responsibilities. We anticipate a rise in ethical considerations and regulatory frameworks focusing on data usage, privacy protection, and the responsible deployment of AI. This will ensure that AI's immense power is harnessed for the greater good, safeguarding against misuse.

The democratization of AI tools presents an exciting prospect, potentially leveling the playing field in cybersecurity. As AI technologies become more accessible, smaller businesses and organizations will also be able to benefit from advanced cybersecurity measures, enhancing overall digital security.

Conversely, the cybersecurity community must prepare for the reality of AI being used for malicious purposes. As AI systems advance, so too do the tactics of cyber attackers, necessitating an ongoing evolution of AI defenses to counteract these emerging threats.

Embracing AI in cybersecurity is a commitment to a safer digital domain. It requires an ongoing effort of staying informed, ethical, and proactive. By striking a balance between leveraging AI's strengths and understanding its limitations, we can harness its potential to forge a more secure digital environment. The journey ahead, filled with both challenges and opportunities, promises to reshape the landscape of cybersecurity in significant ways.

# Appendices

# **F**urther Reading and Resources
### Books:

   i. "Cybersecurity and Cyberwar: What Everyone Needs to Know" by P.W. Singer and Allan Friedman; A comprehensive guide to understanding cybersecurity in the modern world, written in an accessible manner for non-experts.

  ii. "Artificial Intelligence for Cybersecurity" by Anand R. Prasad; This book delves into how AI is shaping the future of cybersecurity, presenting concepts in a clear and straightforward way.

 iii. "Data and Goliath: The Hidden Battles to Collect Your Data and Control Your World" by Bruce Schneier; Schneier's work offers an insightful look into data privacy and security, making complex ideas understandable for a general audience.

**Online Courses:**

   i. Coursera – "AI in Cybersecurity"

An online course that explores the role of AI in cybersecurity. Suitable for beginners, it breaks down complex AI concepts into easy-to-understand modules.

   i. edX – "Cybersecurity Fundamentals"

This course provides an overview of key cybersecurity principles. It's designed for those new to the field and explains concepts in simple terms.

**Websites and Online Resources:**

Krebs on Security (krebsonsecurity.com); A blog by journalist Brian Krebs, offering insightful commentary on cybersecurity issues in an accessible format.

# **About the Author**

Valarian Couch is an esteemed cybersecurity expert, mastering the art of safeguarding against evolving cyber threats. With over 15 years of experience, Valarian has a proven track record in enhancing IT infrastructure security and performance. He is known for his innovative solutions, contributing significantly to improvements in cost savings and user retention.

A passionate advocate for digital privacy and online safety, Valarian's expertise extends beyond professional realms, enriching the global community through insightful writings and unwavering support for open-source initiatives. A respected leader, Valarian excels in fostering team collaboration and exceeding organizational goals.

www.ingramcontent.com/pod-product-compliance
Lightning Source LLC
Chambersburg PA
CBHW031424150726
47989CB00002B/786